cooking to impress

cooking to impress

This edition first published in the U.K. in 1999 by Hamlyn for WHSmith, Greenbridge Road, Swindon SN3 3LD

Octopus Publishing Group Limited
2–4 Heron Quays
London E14 4JP

ISBN 0 600 59888 8

Printed in China

Notes

1 Standard level spoon measurements are used in all recipes.

1 tablespoon = one 15 ml spoon
1 teaspoon = one 5 ml spoon

2 Both imperial and metric measurements have been given in all recipes. Use one set of measurements only and not a mixture of both.

3 Measurements for canned foods have been given as a standard metric equivalent.

4 Eggs should be medium unless otherwise stated. The Department of Health advises that eggs should not be consumed raw. This book may contain dishes made with lightly cooked eggs. It is prudent for more vulnerable people, such as pregnant and nursing mothers, invalids, the elderly, babies and young children, to avoid uncooked or lightly cooked dishes made with eggs. Once prepared, these dishes should be used immediately.

5 Milk should be full fat unless otherwise stated.

6 Poultry should always be cooked thoroughly. To test if poultry is cooked, pierce the flesh through the thickest part with a skewer or fork – the juices should run clear, never pink or red.

7 Fresh herbs should be used unless otherwise stated. If unavailable, use dried herbs as an alternative but halve the quantities stated.

8 Pepper should be freshly ground black pepper unless otherwise stated; season according to taste.

9 Ovens should be preheated to the specified temperature – if using a fan-assisted oven, follow the manufacturer's instructions for adjusting the time and the temperature.

10 Do not re-freeze a dish that has been frozen previously.

11 This book includes dishes made with nuts and nut derivatives. It is advisable for customers with known allergic reactions to nuts and nut derivatives and those who may be potentially vulnerable to these allergies, such as pregnant and nursing mothers, invalids, the elderly, babies and young children, to avoid dishes made with nuts and nut oils. It is also prudent to check the labels of pre-prepared ingredients for the possible inclusion of nut derivatives.

12 Vegetarians should look for the 'V' symbol on a cheese to ensure it is made with vegetarian rennet. There are vegetarian forms of Parmesan, feta, Cheddar, Cheshire, red Leicester, dolcelatte and many goats' cheeses, among others.

contents

6

introduction

Cooking to impress means going to more trouble than usual, spending a bit more time in the kitchen, buying top-quality ingredients and creating a warm and welcoming atmosphere for your guests – putting on a show, in fact. With *Cooking to Impress*, you will be able to create impressive and delicious dishes with ease by following the clear and consise instructions. You may even impress yourself!

Menu Planning

The first step, whether you are planning an intimate meal for two or a large formal dinner party, is to work out your menu, which should be something out of the ordinary and not part of everyday fare. Aim for a balance of colour, texture, flavour and variety, and hot and cold food. You don't want fish, for example, in both the main course and the starter, or too many dishes that look the same; cauliflower soup, creamy chicken risotto and homemade vanilla ice cream served on white plates may taste delicious but the overall whiteness can be somewhat bland. Nor do you want too much pastry – not boeuf en croûte and apple pie, or a savoury mousse for a starter and a sweet one to end the meal.

Choose your main course first. It could depend on the time of the year – spring lamb at Easter time or game like pheasant or partridge as soon as it comes into season, or perhaps a classic and well-tried favourite such as Burgundy-style Beef, Lobster Thermidor or Duck with Orange. Choose a starter that doesn't compete with the main course, but rather works harmoniously with it. A light fish dish such as Ceviche of Salmon gets the gastric juices working while Wild Mushroom Feuilleté has equal appeal to vegetarians and to those with a taste for nature's wild bounty, presented in a sophisticated pastry wrapper. Then think about the dessert, not forgetting the appeal of a well-chosen selection of cheeses to follow. You could consider Red Fruit Salad with Coeurs à la Crème – two treats combined on a single plate – or succumb to the perennial siren song of champagne or chocolate. Both Champagne Summer Berries and Lemon Tart will have your guests coming back for more, as will old favourites such as Chocolate Chip Ice Cream and Chocolate & Cinnamon Bread & Butter Pudding. Finally, don't forget to leave room for a serious piece of indulgence in the shape of homemade Chocolate Truffles to serve with the coffee and liqueurs.

Next, choose your drinks. Is this to be an informal supper party with a simple choice of red or white wine throughout the meal, or do you want a progression from cocktails and aperitifs, through white and red wines, to a dessert wine with the pudding and liqueurs with coffee? And, of course, remember to stock up on soft drinks for drivers, and mixers, fruit juices, and still and sparkling mineral water. It is equally important to chill the white wines, to ensure that the red wines have had time to breathe and are at room temperature, and to make sure that you have a plentiful supply of ice cubes.

1077

'The hostess must be like a duck – calm and unruffled on the surface and paddling like hell underneath.'

Anonymous

8

Getting Ahead

One golden rule of entertaining is never to serve any dish that you aren't confident about. If you and your guests are to enjoy your meal, you mustn't make it difficult for yourself. Remember that practice makes perfect so try out new dishes on friends or family, several times if necessary, before serving them on a special occasion. Another rule is to plan a menu that doesn't involve you spending too much time in the kitchen at the last minute; make as much use of the refrigerator and freezer beforehand as you can. Make detailed shopping lists, do your shopping well ahead, and work out a countdown to make the most sensible and practical use of your time, so that there are no last-minute panics.

Cooking to impress is only one part of the overall picture of entertaining with style. And what this really means is making a social occasion run smoothly, with the addition of a certain amount of panache, to make it go with a swing. Use candles for a softer lighting, select the tablecloth and napkins, clean the silver, polish the glasses, and arrange the flowers, the day before if you can, and then forget all about them.

When it comes to the meal itself, remember that attention to detail shows. Buy the best quality, freshest ingredients that you can afford, make your own mayonnaise, add decorative fruit and vegetable garnishes to your dishes and choose a really good coffee to make even the end of the meal a treat.

Entertaining is all about adding that little something special and having a good time – so, having made all preparations, just relax and enjoy!

Decorating Tricks

Cucumber, Orange and Lemon Slices
To make these classic garnishes look especially decorative, add a fluted edge. Take a 7 cm (3 inch) chunk of cucumber and, holding a canelle knife firmly, use the notch to remove strips of skin at regular intervals down the cucumber, then cut the cucumber into even slices. Oranges and lemons can be prepared in the same way and the pips removed when you slice the fruit.

Frosted Fruit
Small berries and grapes make an excellent decoration for desserts. Wash the fruit carefully and dry it on kitchen paper, then brush it lightly with beaten egg white and dip it into caster sugar. Leave it to dry for 15 minutes on non-stick silicone paper.

mayonnaise

1 Put the egg yolks into a bowl with the vinegar and mustard. Add about ½ teaspoon salt and a generous pinch of pepper and beat well until you have a smooth paste.

2 Gradually beat in the olive oil, adding it drop by drop to begin with. When the mixture begins to thicken, pour in the oil in a thin steady stream, beating well until all the oil has been incorporated.

3 Alternatively, combine the egg yolks, vinegar and mustard in a food processor or blender, then slowly add the oil through the feeder tube, drop by drop at first, then in a steady stream until it is all absorbed and the mayonnaise is thick and creamy.

2 egg yolks

1 tablespoon white wine vinegar

1 teaspoon Dijon mustard

300 ml (½ pint) olive oil

salt and pepper

Makes about 325 ml (11 fl oz)

soups & starters

1 ripe avocado

6 slices of Parma ham, about 75 g (3 oz)

Dressing:

1 tablespoon olive oil

1 teaspoon lemon juice

1 garlic clove, crushed

2 teaspoons chopped parsley

salt and pepper

1 Cut the avocado in half and remove the stone. Peel off the skin and cut each half into 3 thick slices. Wrap 1 slice of ham around each slice of avocado. Arrange on a serving dish or individual dishes.

2 Place all the dressing ingredients in a screw-topped jar and shake well to mix. To serve, pour the dressing over the avocados.

Serves 2

Preparation time: 10 minutes

parma ham with avocado

■ To preserve the colour of cut avocado flesh, rub with a little lemon juice. Handle an avocado carefully as they tend to bruise easily.

15 g (½ oz) butter or margarine

3 sheets of filo pastry

Filling:

3 quail's eggs

40 g (1½ oz) cream cheese

1 tablespoon grated Parmesan cheese

a little cayenne pepper

quail's egg tartlets

To Garnish:

chervil sprigs

salad leaves

1 Melt the butter or margarine and use a little to brush two 7.5 cm (3 inch) tartlet tins.

2 Place the first sheet of filo pastry on a board (keep the rest covered with a damp cloth so they do not dry out). Brush with a little melted butter or margarine, add the second sheet and brush again, then add the third sheet and brush again. Cut six rounds from the triple thickness and press into the tins. Bake in a preheated oven, 200°C (400°F), Gas Mark 6, for about 5 minutes. Allow to cool.

3 Put the eggs into boiling water and cook for 2 minutes. Allow to cool slightly, then cut in half.

4 Meanwhile, blend the cream and Parmesan, adding a shake of cayenne. Spoon into the pastry cases and top with the halved eggs. Sprinkle with more cayenne pepper. Garnish with chervil and a little salad.

Serves 2
Preparation time: 15 minutes
Cooking time: 5 minutes

wild mushroom feuilleté

250 g (8 oz) frozen puff pastry, defrosted

5 g (¼ oz) butter or margarine

250 g (8 oz) closed cup mushrooms, sliced

175 g (6 oz) oyster mushrooms, sliced

150 ml (¼ pint) soured cream

150 ml (¼ pint) single cream

1 garlic clove, crushed

salt and pepper

Serves 2
Preparation time: 20 minutes
Cooking time: 10–12 minutes

1 Roll out the pastry to about 5 mm (¼ inch) thick and cut out three 12 cm (5 inch) circles and three 7 cm (3 inch) ones. Place the circles on a baking sheet and bake in a preheated oven, 230°C (450°F), Gas Mark 8, for 10–12 minutes, until puffed up and golden brown.

2 Meanwhile, melt the butter or margarine and fry the closed cup mushrooms for 3 minutes. Add the oyster mushrooms and cook for 2 minutes until tender. Remove the mushrooms with a slotted spoon and boil the remaining liquid rapidly until reduced to about ½ tablespoon. Add the mushrooms, soured and single creams, garlic and salt and pepper. Reheat gently without boiling.

3 To serve, place some mushroom mixture and liquid on top of each large pastry circle. Cover each with a smaller pastry circle and serve.

■ Most supermarkets now carry a large selection of wild mushrooms. Look for ceps, morels, chanterelles and horse mushrooms as well.

ceviche of salmon

1 Cut the salmon fillet into very thin slices – about the same thickness as sliced smoked salmon. Arrange the raw salmon on two plates in a single layer.

2 Sprinkle the salmon with lemon juice and olive oil, and season to taste with salt and pepper. Leave to marinate for a minimum of 30 minutes.

3 Garnish with dill or fennel sprigs and serve with bread and butter.

175 g (6 oz) piece of salmon fillet

lemon juice, for sprinkling

olive oil, for sprinkling

salt and pepper

dill or fennel sprigs, to garnish

brown bread and butter, to serve

Serves 2

Preparation time: 20 minutes, plus marinating

pears wrapped in parma ham

1 Cut each slice of Parma ham in half lengthways. Cut each pear into 6 wedges and remove the core.

2 Wrap a piece of Parma ham around each pear wedge and thread 3 wedges on to each skewer.

3 Place the skewers under a preheated hot grill or on an oiled barbecue grill and cook for about 2–3 minutes on each side. Serve hot on a bed of salad leaves. Using a vegetable peeler, shave the Parmesan over the skewers, sprinkle with pepper and drizzle with a little olive oil.

2 ripe pears

6 slices Parma ham

To Serve:

salad leaves

shavings of Parmesan cheese

pepper

extra virgin olive oil

Preparation time: 10 minutes

Cooking time: 4–6 minutes

Serves 4

oysters in cream sauce

12 fresh oysters in shell, opened, rinsed and liquor strained and reserved

dry white wine, to fill

Cream Sauce:

2 tablespoons unsalted butter

2 spring onions, including green parts, chopped

1 garlic clove, crushed

1 tablespoon flour

50 ml (2 fl oz) dry white wine

Tabasco sauce, to taste

1 egg yolk

50 ml (2 fl oz) double cream

25 g (1 oz) button mushrooms, finely chopped

75 g (3 oz) cooked, peeled prawns, finely chopped

salt and white pepper

20 g (¾ oz) Parmesan cheese, grated

2 tablespoons fine dry breadcrumbs

Serves 2

Preparation time: 15 minutes

Cooking time: 30–40 minutes

---

1 Measure 250 ml (8 fl oz) oyster liquor. Add dry white wine to make up the quantity. Scrub the deeper shell halves and add an oyster to each. Arrange in crumpled foil in a pan. Keep cool.

2 Melt the butter in a saucepan, then add the spring onions and garlic. Cook, stirring, until soft but not brown. Stir in the flour and cook for 1 minute, then gradually stir in the oyster liquor and dry white wine. Bring to the boil, lower the heat and simmer for 15 minutes, stirring constantly. Season to taste with salt and pepper, adding a little Tabasco.

3 Blend the egg yolk and cream. Add 2 tablespoons of the hot sauce, then stir into the remaining sauce in the pan. Gently stir until thickened, without boiling. Remove from the heat and stir in the mushrooms and prawns. Spoon over the oysters.

4 Mix together the Parmesan and breadcrumbs and sprinkle over the tops of the oysters. Bake in a preheated oven, 200°C (400°F), Gas Mark 6, for 15–20 minutes or until golden brown and the edges of the oysters begin to curl. Serve hot.

dressed crab

1 Extract the white and brown meat from the crabs and keep them separate. Tap out the shell of the crab, then wash thoroughly in boiling water and dry with kitchen paper.

2 Lightly season the crab meat with salt and pepper. Separate the yolk and white of the hard-boiled eggs and push them through a sieve.

3 Arrange the brown crab meat down the sides of each shell then place a line of sieved hard-boiled egg white on top. Make a thin strip of chopped parsley followed by the sieved egg yolk. Heap the white crab meat in the centre of the shells and sprinkle with the lemon juice. Top with sieved egg white. Sprinkle the paprika between the egg yolk and the egg white. Serve each crab on a bed of salad leaves with mayonnaise, lemon wedges and thin slices of brown bread and butter.

2 cooked crabs, about 750 g (1½ lb) each

2 hard-boiled eggs

4 tablespoons finely chopped flat leaf parsley

a few drops of lemon juice

paprika pepper

salt and pepper

To Serve:

mixed salad leaves

mayonnaise (see page 9)

lemon wedges

brown bread and butter

Serves 4

Preparation time: 40 minutes

---

1 Extract the brown and white meat from the crab and keep them separate. Put the shells in a plastic bag and, using a rolling pin, smash into small pieces. Place the shells in a large saucepan, with any asparagus trimmings, and cover with 1.2 litres (2 pints) of the water. Bring to the boil, reduce the heat and simmer gently for 30 minutes. Strain through a fine sieve into a clean pan.

2 Place the remaining water in a saucepan with a pinch of salt, bring to the boil, add the asparagus and simmer for 2–3 minutes until just tender. Drain, reserving the liquid, refresh the asparagus in cold water, drain again and set aside. Bring the crab stock back to the boil, add the asparagus water, reduce the heat and add the rice. Simmer gently for 12–15 minutes until the rice is cooked.

3 Place the cream cheese in a bowl with 5 tablespoons of the brown crab meat. Season with salt, pepper and cayenne and mix well. Toast the bread on both sides until lightly golden. Spread with the crab meat mixture and keep warm.

4 Reduce the heat under the stock to a minimum. Mix the egg yolks and 2 tablespoons of the lemon juice in a bowl and whisk in a ladleful of the hot stock. Whisk the egg mixture back into the stock; do not let it boil or it will curdle. Season to taste, adding more lemon juice if required. Add the reserved asparagus and white crab meat and heat through. Serve at once, sprinkled with the chervil sprigs and accompanied by the crab toasts.

crab, asparagus & lemon soup

1 crab, about 750 g (1½ lb)

250 g (8 oz) fine young asparagus, trimmed and cut into 5 cm (2 inch) pieces

1.65 litres (2¾ pints) water

75 g (3 oz) long-grain rice

50 g (2 oz) cream cheese

cayenne pepper

8 thin slices of French bread

3 egg yolks

2–4 tablespoons lemon juice

salt and pepper

chervil sprigs, to garnish

Serves 4
Preparation time: 25 minutes
Cooking time: 1 hour

smoked oyster tartlets

1 Roll out the dough thinly and cut into rounds with a 6 cm (2½ inch) cutter. Line 12 greased mini tartlet tins with the dough rounds and prick all over with a fork.

2 Bake the pastry cases blind in a preheated oven, 220°C (425°F), Gas Mark 7, for 10 minutes. Remove from the oven and reduce the heat to 190°C (375°F), Gas Mark 5.

3 Divide the oysters and parsley between the pastry cases. Mix together the egg and cream and season to taste with cayenne and pepper. Pour the mixture into the pastry cases and bake the tarts for a further 15–20 minutes or until the filling is set and golden brown.

250 g (8 oz) shortcrust pastry

50 g (2 oz) smoked oysters, drained and chopped

1 teaspoon chopped parsley

1 egg

150 ml (¼ pint) pint single cream

pinch of cayenne pepper

pepper

Makes about 12	
Preparation time: 20 minutes	
Cooking time: 30 minutes	

■ Baking blind is a method of partially prebaking the pastry before a filling, which does not require the same amount of baking or might soak into uncooked pastry, is added.

smoked salmon timbales

1 Oil 4 timbale moulds. Line them with smoked salmon, and chop any leftover salmon into small pieces. Mix together the taramasalata, cheese, Tabasco sauce, lemon juice and cayenne pepper. Add the chopped leftover salmon. Divide the mixture between the moulds. Level the tops and chill well for 2–3 hours.

2 Carefully turn the timbales out of the moulds and serve garnished with lemon slices and dill sprigs.

■ If you don't have any timbale moulds, baba and dariole moulds or small ramekins can be used in the same way.

1 tablespoon sunflower oil, for greasing

175 g (6 oz) smoked salmon, thinly sliced

175 g (6 oz) taramasalata

175 g (6 oz) full fat soft cheese

dash of Tabasco sauce

juice of ½ lemon

pinch of cayenne pepper

To Garnish:

lemon slices

dill sprigs

Serves 4

Preparation time: 15 minutes, plus chilling

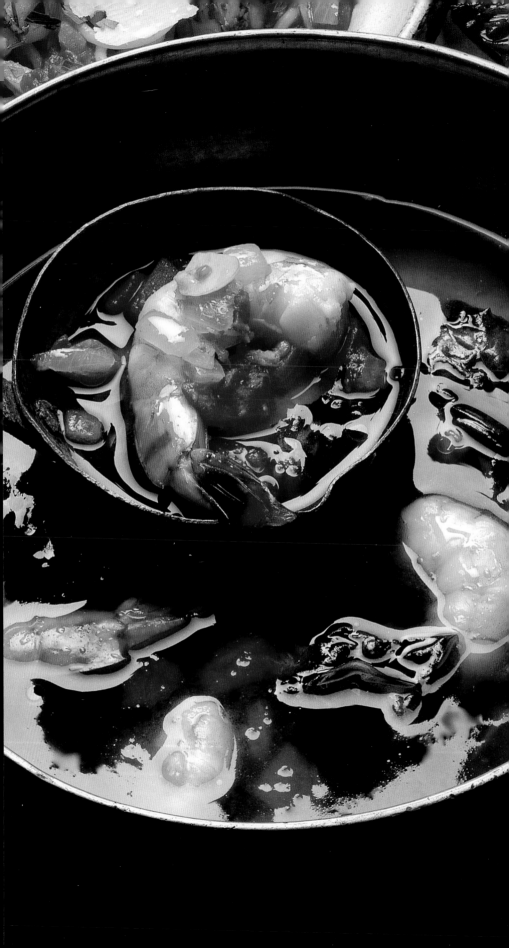

500 g (1 lb) raw tiger prawns

1 red chilli, bruised

3 lemon grass stalks, roughly chopped, or grated rind of 2 lemons

1 tablespoon grated lime rind

4 slices of fresh root ginger

2 coriander sprigs

900 ml (1½ pints) vegetable stock

2 tablespoons sunflower oil

1 small onion, chopped

2 garlic cloves, sliced

1 teaspoon grated fresh root ginger

2 x 400 g (13 oz) cans chopped tomatoes

2 tablespoons light soy sauce

12 basil leaves

1 Peel the prawns, reserve the meat and place the heads and shells in a large heavy-based pan. Add the chilli, lemon grass or lemon rind, lime rind, sliced root ginger, coriander and stock. Bring to the boil, cover and simmer gently for 30 minutes.

2 Heat the oil in a large pan and fry the onion, garlic and grated ginger for 5 minutes. Add the tomatoes and simmer for a further 5 minutes. Strain the prawn shell stock and add it to the tomatoes with the soy sauce; bring to the boil, cover and simmer gently for 10 minutes. Add the prawns and simmer for a further 5–6 minutes or until cooked. Serve in bowls topped with the basil.

Serves 4

Preparation time: 20 minutes

Cooking time: 1 hour

thai tomato & prawn broth

■ Light soy sauce is generally more salty and used for cooking, while the thicker and sweeter dark soy sauce is better for dipping.

thai prawn parcels

1 Place the garlic, shallot, ginger, lemon grass, lime rind, chilli flakes, chilli oil, fish sauce, lime juice and sugar in a food processor or blender and grind to a thick paste. Add the coconut milk and mix well.

2 Place the prawns in a bowl and add the coconut spice mixture. Stir to coat the prawns evenly. Butter 4 large pieces of greaseproof paper. Place 6 prawns and a quarter of the coconut mixture in the centre of each piece. Wrap up to enclose the prawns, forming neat parcels. Steam the prawn parcels over a pan of boiling water for 8–10 minutes.

3 To serve, unwrap the prawns and place them on plates lined with pieces of banana leaf, if liked. Pour the coconut mixture into a bowl and whisk briefly until smooth. Pour a little over each portion and garnish with spring onions and red pepper strips.

2 garlic cloves

1 shallot, chopped

5 cm (2 inch) piece of fresh root ginger, peeled and chopped

1 lemon grass stalk, finely chopped

2 teaspoons grated lime rind

1 teaspoon dried red chilli flakes

2 teaspoons chilli oil

1 tablespoon fish sauce (nam pla)

1 tablespoon lime juice

¼ teaspoon caster sugar

75 ml (3 fl oz) coconut milk

24 raw prawns, peeled and deveined, tails left intact

To Garnish:

spring onions, sliced into strips

½ red pepper, cored, deseeded and sliced into thin strips

Serves 4

Preparation time: 30 minutes

Cooking time: 8–10 minutes

globe artichokes with garlic & herb mayonnaise

1 First make the garlic and herb mayonnaise. Put the mayonnaise into a bowl, stir in the garlic and mixed herbs and leave to stand for at least 30 minutes.

2 Discard the large base stalks from the artichokes and rub the cut surface with lemon to prevent discolouring. Put the artichokes in a large pan of boiling water. Squeeze the juice from the lemon quarters into the pan and drop the pieces in too. Cook the artichokes for 25–30 minutes, until a leaf can be pulled out easily. Using a slotted spoon, remove the artichokes and leave upside down to drain and cool slightly.

3 Cut each artichoke into 4 wedges. Discard the hairy choke. Arrange the artichoke quarters on individual plates or a large platter. Drizzle the olive oil over, and add salt and pepper. Serve with garlic and herb mayonnaise for dipping. Garnish with lemon wedges.

4 globe artichokes

1 lemon, quartered

4 tablespoons olive oil

salt and pepper

Garlic & Herb Mayonnaise:

300 ml (10 fl oz) ready-made mayonnaise (or see page 9)

2 garlic cloves, crushed

2 tablespoons finely chopped mixed tarragon, chives and parsley

lemon wedges, to garnish

Serves 4

Preparation time: 15 minutes, plus standing

Cooking time: 25–30 minutes

classic paella ●

mussels in white wine sauce ●

pan-fried salmon with tomato coulis ●

lobster & asparagus salad ●

monkfish & vegetable parcels with saffron sauce ●

lobster thermidor ●

trout with almonds ●

skate in orange & cider sauce ●

seafood risotto ●

sole bonne femme ●

normandy-style sole ●

salmon with three sauces ●

thai steamed fish curry ●

fish &
shellfish

classic paella

1 Put the garlic slices in a large pan with the herbs, wine, 150 ml (¼ pint) of the stock and season with salt and pepper. Add the mussels, cover the pan tightly and bring to the boil. Shake the pan and simmer for 5 minutes until the mussels open. Remove the mussels and set aside, discarding any which remain closed. Strain the liquid and reserve.

2 Heat half of the oil in a saucepan and fry the squid for 5 minutes, stirring frequently. Add the onion, red pepper and crushed garlic and cook gently, stirring frequently, for 5 minutes. Add the mussel liquid and tomatoes and season. Bring to the boil then simmer, stirring, for 15–20 minutes until thick. Transfer to a bowl.

3 Heat the remaining oil in a large sauté pan and fry the chicken for 5 minutes. Add the rice and turn it in the oil for 3 minutes. Stir in the squid mixture. Add about one-third of the remaining stock and bring to the boil, stirring constantly. Boil rapidly for about 3–4 minutes, then cover the pan and simmer for 30 minutes. Add more stock as the rice becomes dry and stir frequently. The paella is ready when the chicken is cooked, the rice is tender but still firm and almost all the liquid has been absorbed.

4 Add the peas and prawns, if using, and simmer, stirring, for 5 minutes or until cooked, adding more stock if required. Arrange the mussels on top of the paella, cover the pan tightly with foil and cook for 5 minutes or until the mussels are hot. Serve garnished with the parsley.

4 garlic cloves, (2 sliced, 2 crushed)

1 bunch of fresh mixed herbs

150 ml (¼ pint) dry white wine

2 litres (3½ pints) hot chicken stock

1 kg (2 lb) fresh mussels, cleaned (see page 32)

4 tablespoons virgin olive oil

4 small squid, cleaned and sliced into rings

1 large onion, finely chopped

1 red pepper, cored, deseeded and chopped

4 large ripe tomatoes, skinned, deseeded and chopped

12 skinned and boned chicken thighs, cut into bite-sized pieces

500 g (1 lb) arborio rice

125 g (4 oz) fresh or frozen peas

12 large raw prawns, peeled (optional)

salt and pepper

To Garnish:

1 tablespoon chopped flat leaf parsley

parsley sprigs

Serves 6
Preparation time: about 40 minutes
Cooking time: about 1¼ hours

mussels in white wine sauce

1 Scrub the mussels with a stiff brush and scrape off the beards and barnacles with a small sharp knife. Discard any open mussels.

2 Melt half the butter in a large heavy-based pan and gently fry the onion, garlic and leek until soft but not coloured. Add the mussels, wine and water, cover and bring to the boil. Cook for 2–5 minutes until the mussels open, shaking the pan several times during the cooking. Divide the mussels between 4 large soup bowls, discarding any that have not opened during cooking. Keep hot.

3 Mix the remaining butter with the flour to form a paste and little by little add to the juices in the pan, stirring to thicken.

4 Bring the mussel liquid to the boil, season with salt and pepper to taste, stir in the parsley and pour over the mussels. For extra richness, 1–2 tablespoons double cream can be added to the sauce just before serving, if liked.

2 kg (4 lb) mussels

50 g (2 oz) butter

1 large onion, finely chopped

1–2 garlic cloves, finely chopped

1 small leek, white and green parts, finely sliced

300 ml (½ pint) dry white wine

150 ml (¼ pint) water

25 g (1 oz) plain flour

2 tablespoons finely chopped flat leaf parsley

1–2 tablespoons double cream (optional)

salt and pepper

Serves 4

Preparation time: 20 minutes

Cooking time: 10 minutes

1 To make the tomato coulis, place all the ingredients, except the lemon juice, in a saucepan and bring to the boil. Reduce the heat, cover and simmer for about 10 minutes until very soft. Remove the bouquet garni.

2 Purée the coulis in a food processor, then press it through a sieve. Return to the boil and reduce to a sauce-like consistency. Add the lemon juice and season to taste.

3 Heat the oil in a frying pan and sauté the garlic for a few minutes to flavour the oil, then discard the garlic. Season the salmon with salt, pepper and nutmeg, add to the pan, and sauté at high heat for a few seconds on each side. Reduce the heat and cook for a few minutes until the fish is cooked through. Remove and keep warm. Pour the wine into the pan, stir to mix with the juices, then pour the contents into the coulis.

4 Serve the salmon with salad leaves and dill sprigs, and spoon the tomato coulis beside it.

1 tablespoon olive oil

1 garlic clove, crushed

2 fresh salmon steaks or cutlets

ground nutmeg, to taste

½ small glass red wine (optional)

salt and pepper

Tomato Coulis:

750 g (1½ lb) ripe tomatoes, sliced

1 small onion, finely chopped

a pinch of sugar

1 bouquet garni

juice of ½ lemon

salt and pepper

To Serve:

mixed salad leaves

dill sprigs

Serves 2
Preparation time: 20 minutes
Cooking time: 10–15 minutes

pan-fried salmon with tomato coulis

lobster & asparagus salad

1 First make the dressing. Put the garlic, anchovies and herbs into a food processor and blend well. Add the mayonnaise and process to mix. Add the vinegar and salt and pepper to taste. Turn into a bowl, cover and chill for at least 1 hour. Before serving, stir in a few tablespoons of soured cream, if liked.

2 Trim the ends from the asparagus spears, making them all the same length. Then, if necessary, scrape the sides of each spear with a swivel-bladed vegetable parer, starting about 5 cm (2 inches) from the tip. Cook the asparagus in a pan of salted boiling water for 4–8 minutes, depending on size, or until tender but still crisp. Drain and refresh under cold running water, then drain again. Leave to cool.

3 Crack the claws and tails of the lobsters and remove the meat. Keep the claw meat whole, and slice the tail meat across into neat rounds.

4 Arrange the asparagus spears and lobster meat on a bed of salad leaves. Spoon over a little of the dressing and serve the rest separately.

500 g (1 lb) asparagus spears

2 lobsters, 500–750 g (1–1½ lb) each, freshly cooked

mixed salad leaves, to serve

Herb Dressing:

1 small garlic clove, crushed

2 anchovies, well drained

1 tablespoon snipped chives

1 tablespoon chopped parsley

1 teaspoon chopped tarragon

125 ml (4 fl oz) mayonnaise

1 teaspoon tarragon vinegar

a few tablespoons soured cream (optional)

salt and pepper

Serves 2

Preparation time: 20 minutes, plus chilling

Cooking time: 5 minutes

monkfish & vegetable parcels with saffron sauce

500 g (1 lb) monkfish, skinned and boned

2 carrots, cut into matchsticks

2 celery sticks, cut into matchsticks

1 onion, very finely sliced into half rings

1 red pepper, cored, deseeded and cut into matchsticks

2 tablespoons lemon juice

3 tablespoons white wine

salt and pepper

flat leaf parsley sprigs, to garnish

1 To make the saffron sauce, put the wine in a small saucepan, add the shallot and boil until the wine is reduced to about ½ tablespoon. Remove from the heat, stir in the cream and saffron and set aside.

2 Cut out four large pieces of foil and lightly butter them. Cut the monkfish into medallions. Arrange a few medallions in the centre of each piece of foil and surround them with small bundles of the prepared vegetables. Sprinkle with the lemon juice and wine, and season lightly with salt and pepper. Bring the corners of the foil together and crimp the edges so that the parcels are totally sealed.

3 Place the parcels in a steamer over a pan of boiling water, and steam for about 10 minutes, or until the fish is tender.

4 Open the parcels and pour a quarter of the saffron sauce over each portion of fish – the juices and sauce mingle and taste delicious. Serve hot, garnished with parsley sprigs.

Saffron Sauce:

75 ml (3 fl oz) dry white wine

1 shallot, finely chopped

75 ml (3 fl oz) double cream

pinch of powdered saffron

Serves 4
Preparation time: 20 minutes
Cooking time: about 20 minutes

lobster thermidor

1 Cut the lobster lengthways in half and remove the meat from the shell. Cut it up into pieces about 1 cm (½ inch) long (you will find this easier if you cut the meat at an angle). Wash and dry the shells. Heat half the butter in a small frying pan and add the lobster. Fry gently, turning occasionally.

2 Meanwhile, heat the remaining butter in a small pan, add the onion and fry gently until soft. Add the flour and blend thoroughly. Add the milk to the pan, stirring, and bring to the boil. Simmer for a few minutes, then add the Cheddar. Mix thoroughly over a low heat, then add the wine and paprika. Season with salt and pepper.

3 Pour the sauce over the lobster in the frying pan and mix well. Cook over a low heat for a few minutes. Place the cleaned lobster shells on a grill rack, then spoon the lobster mixture into them. Sprinkle thickly with Parmesan and place under a preheated grill. Cook until the sauce is bubbling and golden brown. Arrange a bed of salad leaves on 2 serving plates, place the lobster on top and garnish with lemon wedges.

1 kg (2 lb) lobster, cooked

50 g (2 oz) butter

1 small onion, finely chopped

25 g (1 oz) plain flour

150 ml (¼ pint) milk

25 g (1 oz) Cheddar cheese, grated

1 tablespoon white wine

a pinch of paprika pepper

2 tablespoons grated Parmesan cheese

salt and pepper

To Garnish:

salad leaves

lemon wedges

Serves 2

Preparation time: 45 minutes

Cooking time: 20 minutes

■ It is not easy to cut a lobster neatly in half, so ask your fishmonger to do it for you.

trout with almonds

1 Season the flour with salt and pepper and dust over the trout.

2 Heat half of the butter in a large pan and fry the trout for about 3–4 minutes on each side. Remove the trout from the pan and keep warm.

3 Add the rest of the butter to the frying pan with the flaked almonds and fry gently until the almonds have turned golden. Add the lemon juice and season to taste with salt and pepper, then heat the sauce thoroughly and pour over the trout. Garnish with fennel sprigs and lemon wedges and serve at once.

plain flour, for coating

4 medium trout, cleaned

125 g (4 oz) butter

125 g (4 oz) flaked almonds

2 tablespoons lemon juice

salt and pepper

To Garnish:

fennel sprigs

lemon wedges

Serves 4
Preparation time: 15 minutes
Cooking time: about 20 minutes

skate in orange & cider sauce

1 Place the skate wings in a large shallow pan. Add the onion, cider, orange juice and rind, then a pinch of salt and pepper. Bring slowly up to a barely simmering point and poach for about 15 minutes.

2 Lift out the skate wings with a slotted spoon, place them on a warmed serving dish and keep warm.

3 Turn up the heat, add the capers and boil the cooking liquor until it is reduced and thick, then taste and adjust the seasoning if necessary. Add a squeeze of lemon juice, remove from the heat and swirl in the cream. Pour the sauce over the skate and serve immediately, garnished with the orange segments. Serve with green vegetables, if liked.

4 skate wings

1 small onion, finely chopped

300 ml (½ pint) dry cider

juice and finely pared rind of 1 orange

salt and pepper

1 tablespoon capers

a squeeze of lemon juice

4 tablespoons double cream

orange segments, peeled and quartered, to garnish

Serves 4
Preparation time: 15 minutes
Cooking time: 20 minutes

■ The delicate shape and texture of the skate wing makes it perfect to serve for a special meal. Skate is best poached, steamed or shallow fried.

1 To prepare the seafood, wash and clean the octopus or squid and slice them into rings. Cut the tentacles into small pieces. Wash, peel and devein the prawns. Cut the fish into large chunks.

2 Heat the oil in a large pan and fry the onion and garlic gently until soft and golden. Add the rice and stir for 1–2 minutes.

3 Add some of the stock and the chopped tomatoes and bring to the boil. Reduce the heat and simmer gently, stirring in more stock as and when necessary, until all the liquid has been absorbed and the rice is tender. After 15 minutes, add the prepared seafood. Stir in the parsley and season with salt and pepper when the rice is cooked.

4 Cut the chillies into thin strips and use as a garnish. Serve the risotto with lime wedges.

1 kg (2 lb) mixed seafood (octopus, squid, prawns, white fish)

2 tablespoons olive oil

1 large onion, chopped

2 garlic cloves, crushed

250 g (8 oz) arborio rice

600–750 ml (1–1½ pints) fish stock

3 tomatoes, skinned and chopped

2 tablespoons finely chopped flat leaf parsley

salt and pepper

To Serve:

4 red or green chillies

lime wedges

Serves 4	
Preparation time: 15 minutes	
Cooking time: 45 minutes	

seafood risotto

sole bonne femme

75 g (3 oz) butter

4 shallots, chopped

125 g (4 oz) mushrooms, sliced

2 tablespoons chopped parsley

1 kg (2 lb) sole fillets, halved lengthways and skinned

4 tablespoons dry white wine

150 ml (¼ pint) fish stock

2 tablespoons lemon juice

25 g (1 oz) plain flour

salt and pepper

To Garnish:

parsley sprigs

lemon twists

Serves 4–6
Preparation time: 20 minutes
Cooking time: about 30 minutes

1 Melt 50 g (2 oz) of the butter in a saucepan and shallow-fry the shallots and mushrooms. Stir in the parsley, then spread the mixture evenly over the base of an ovenproof, flameproof dish.

2 Roll up the sole fillets from head to tail, put them into the dish and season well with salt and pepper. Pour over the white wine, stock and lemon juice and bake in a preheated oven, 180°C (350°F), Gas Mark 4, for 15 minutes.

3 Transfer the sole to a warmed serving dish and place the dish in which it was cooked over a medium heat on the hob. Mix the remaining butter with the flour to form a paste. Add it in small knobs to the boiling mushroom mixture and whisk until the butter melts and the sauce thickens.

4 Pour the sauce over the sole and serve hot, garnished with parsley and lemon and a selection of seasonal green vegetables.

normandy-style sole

1 Season the fillets with salt and pepper. Melt 25 g (1 oz) of the butter in a flameproof casserole, add the fillets and mushrooms, sprinkle with the lemon juice and pour in the hot stock. Cover and bake in a preheated oven, 180°C (350°F), Gas Mark 4, for 12–15 minutes, until the sole is tender. Remove the fish and mushrooms and keep warm. Reserve the stock.

2 Put the mussels into a large saucepan with the shallots and wine. Cook over a high heat until the shells open, shaking the pan. Discard any that do not open. Remove half of the mussels from their shells. Keep all the mussels warm. Strain the cooking juices from the mussels and the sole into a pan and boil steadily until reduced by three-quarters. Remove from the heat.

3 Mix together the egg yolks and cream and stir into the cooking juices. Cook over a low heat, stirring, for 3–4 minutes; do not boil. Remove from the heat and whisk in the remaining butter, a little at a time.

4 Arrange the sole fillets, shelled mussels and prawns on four warmed plates. Pour over the sauce and garnish with the mussels in their shells, chopped parsley, parsley sprigs and lemon slices.

4 x 300 g (10 oz) Dover soles, filleted

150 g (5 oz) butter

125 g (4 oz) mushrooms

1 tablespoon lemon juice

600 ml (1 pint) hot fish stock

1 kg (2 lb) mussels, cleaned (see page 32)

4 shallots, finely chopped

150 ml (¼ pint) dry white wine

2 egg yolks

200 ml (7 fl oz) double cream

125 g (4 oz) cooked peeled prawns

salt and pepper

To Garnish:

2 tablespoons chopped parsley

parsley sprigs

lemon slices

Serves 4

Preparation time: 15 minutes

Cooking time: 1 hour

salmon with three sauces

1 Wash the salmon belly cavity, then pat dry with kitchen paper and season lightly with salt and pepper. Grease a sheet of foil with the butter. Put the salmon on the foil, wrap it up and place in a baking dish. Bake in a preheated oven, 150°C (300°F), Gas Mark 2, for about 1 hour. Remove from the oven and leave to cool.

2 Meanwhile, prepare the sauces. To make the avocado sauce, place the avocado, yogurt, salt and pepper, and lemon juice to taste in a food processor and blend until smooth. To make the other sauces, mix the ingredients together, season and chill until ready to serve.

3 Remove the salmon carefully from the foil and put it on a large chopping board. Using a thin-bladed sharp knife, cut through the skin along the backbone, across the tail and around the head. Using the knife blade, remove the skin and the fins. With the back of the knife, scrape away the brown-coloured flesh in the centre. Turn the salmon over and repeat. Then cut down along the backbone of the fish, turn the knife flat and ease the fillet gently from the bone, and lift off. (This may have to be done in two pieces.) At the head and tail, cut through the bone with kitchen scissors and peel away. Replace the upper fillet. Slice the salmon into portions.

4 Place a slice of salmon on each plate and pour pools of the sauces next to it. Garnish with cucumber and lemon slices, and dill and chervil.

1 salmon, about 2 kg (4 lb), cleaned

50 g (2 oz) butter, melted

lettuce leaves, to serve

salt and pepper

Avocado Sauce:

1 ripe avocado, peeled and stoned

150 ml (¼ pint) natural yogurt

2–4 tablespoons lemon juice

Horseradish Sauce:

1–2 tablespoons grated horseradish

150 ml (¼ pint) soured cream

50 g (2 oz) walnuts, chopped

Cocktail Sauce:

1–2 tablespoons tomato ketchup

150 ml (¼ pint) mayonnaise

a few drops of Tabasco sauce

To Garnish:

thin cucumber slices (see page 8)

thin lemon slices (see page 8)

dill sprigs

chervil sprigs

Serves 8–10

Preparation time: about 1 hour, plus chilling

Cooking time: about 1 hour

thai steamed fish curry

1 Mix together the Thai red curry paste, coconut milk, fish sauce and beaten egg. Set aside.

2 Place the fish pieces in a shallow non-metallic dish. Add the coriander, mint and Thai sweet basil and gently mix together. Pour the curry paste mixture over the fish and stir to coat evenly.

3 Scatter the lime rind and chilli slices over the fish. Cover the dish with foil and steam over boiling water for 15 minutes or until the fish is just cooked through. The egg will lightly thicken the sauce. Serve immediately with rice.

3 tablespoons Thai red curry paste

200 ml (7 fl oz) coconut milk

1 tablespoon fish sauce (nam pla)

1 egg, beaten

500 g (1 lb) skinless cod or halibut fillets, cut into 5 cm (2 inch) pieces

1 tablespoon chopped coriander

1 tablespoon chopped mint

1 tablespoon chopped Thai sweet basil

1 tablespoon grated lime rind

1 large green chilli, deseeded and finely sliced

1 large red chilli, deseeded and finely sliced

plain boiled rice, to serve

Serves 4	
Preparation time: 10 minutes	
Cooking time: 15 minutes	

■ Banana leaves add a touch of the exotic when serving Thai meals. Whole leaves can be purchased from Thai or Oriental stores. Dip in boiling water to soften before serving.

vegetables in malaysian coconut sauce •

spinach & mushroom roulade •

mediterranean vegetable salad •

spicy aubergines with tomatoes •

leek terrine with walnuts & feta •

seasonal vegetable medley •

wild mushrooms in crispy cases •

vegetable terrine •

camembert & cranberry pie •

tagliatelle with mushrooms & cream •

wild mushroom salad with croûtons •

vegetarian

1 First make the coconut sauce. Put the tamarind into a bowl. Pour over the boiling water and leave to soak for 30 minutes. Mash the tamarind in the soaking water, then strain through a wire sieve set over a bowl, pressing the tamarind to extract as much pulp as possible.

2 Skim 2 tablespoons of the cream from the coconut milk and place it in a wok or heavy-based saucepan. Add the curry paste, ginger, onion and turmeric and cook over gentle heat, stirring, for 2–3 minutes. Stir in the remaining coconut milk and the tamarind water. Bring to the boil, then lower the heat and season with salt.

3 Add the broccoli to the sauce and cook for 5 minutes, then add the French beans and red pepper, and cook, stirring, for a further 5 minutes. Finally, stir in the courgettes and cook for 1–2 minutes. Prawn crackers make a nice accompaniment.

125 g (4 oz) broccoli florets

125 g (4 oz) French beans, cut into 2.5 cm (1 inch) lengths

1 red pepper, cored, deseeded and sliced

125 g (4 oz) courgettes, thinly sliced

Coconut Sauce:

25 g (1 oz) tamarind pulp

150 ml (¼ pint) boiling water

425 g (14 oz) can thick coconut milk

2 teaspoons Thai green curry paste

1 teaspoon grated ginger

1 onion, diced

½ teaspoon ground turmeric

salt

Serves 4
Preparation time: 15 minutes, plus soaking
Cooking time: about 20 minutes

vegetables in malaysian coconut sauce

■ Tamarind pulp is available from large supermarkets and Asian food stores. Its sweet and sour flavour adds a delicious bite to many dishes. Use lemon juice or vinegar as a substitute.

spinach & mushroom roulade

1 Line a 30 x 20 cm (12 x 8 inch) Swiss roll tin with greaseproof paper and oil lightly, or make a case of the same measurements with aluminium foil. Put the spinach into a saucepan with the knob of butter and cook until soft. Drain the spinach well, chop and transfer to a large bowl. Add the egg yolks, beating them well into the chopped spinach and season to taste with salt and pepper.

2 Whisk the egg whites in a large grease-free bowl until just holding their shape. Using a metal spoon, quickly fold them into the spinach mixture. Spoon the mixture into the prepared Swiss roll tin, sprinkle with the grated Parmesan and bake in a preheated oven, 200°C (400°F), Gas Mark 6, for 10 minutes.

3 Meanwhile, make the filling. Heat the butter in a small saucepan. Add the sliced mushrooms and cook gently until softened. Stir in the flour and cook, stirring constantly, for 1 minute. Slowly stir in the milk and cook the sauce until thickened. Stir in the nutmeg and season to taste.

4 Remove the spinach roulade from the oven and invert on to a sheet of greaseproof paper. Quickly spread the mushroom filling over the surface then gently roll up the roulade. Cut into thick slices and serve immediately with a salad garnish.

500 g (1 lb) fresh spinach

knob of butter

4 eggs, separated

25 g (1 oz) Parmesan cheese, grated

salt and pepper

salad leaves, to garnish

Filling:

15 g (½ oz) butter

175 g (6 oz) closed cap mushrooms, sliced

1 tablespoon plain flour

150 ml (¼ pint) milk

pinch of nutmeg

Serves 4

Preparation time: 15 minutes

Cooking time: about 20 minutes

mediterranean vegetable salad

1 Put the fennel and onions into a large saucepan of boiling water. When the water returns to the boil, cook the vegetables for 1 minute. Add the courgette strips and cook for 1 minute more. Drain in a colander and refresh under cold running water, then drain again and set aside.

2 Combine the olive oil, lemon rind and thyme in a large bowl. Add all the vegetables and toss lightly to coat them in the flavoured oil.

3 Line a grill pan with foil. Spread the vegetable mixture evenly in a single layer in the pan and cook under a preheated hot grill for about 15 minutes, turning frequently, until the vegetables are tender and patched with brown. Leave to cool.

4 To make the dressing, whisk all the ingredients together in a small bowl. Arrange the cooled vegetables on individual plates or a serving platter. Pour the dressing over the vegetables and serve.

2 small fennel bulbs, cut into wedges

2 red onions, cut into wedges

3 courgettes, halved and sliced lengthways into strips

4 tablespoons extra virgin olive oil

1 teaspoon finely grated lemon rind

1 tablespoon chopped thyme

1 red or yellow pepper, cored, deseeded and cut into wide strips

175 g (6 oz) cherry tomatoes, halved

Dressing:

4 tablespoons extra virgin olive oil

2 tablespoons lemon juice

pinch of sugar

1 tablespoon chopped oregano

salt and pepper

Serves 4

Preparation time: 15 minutes

Cooking time: about 25 minutes

750 g (1½ lb) aubergines, cut into 4 cm (1½ inch) chunks

4 tablespoons lemon juice

175 g (6 oz) butter or ghee

2 onions, thinly sliced

4 garlic cloves, thinly sliced

7.5 cm (3 inch) piece of fresh root ginger, peeled and thinly sliced

2 teaspoons black onion seeds

7.5 cm (3 inch) piece of cinnamon stick

2 teaspoons coriander seeds

2 teaspoons cumin seeds

2 teaspoons pepper

2 teaspoons salt

2 teaspoons garam masala

1½ teaspoons ground turmeric

1 teaspoon chilli powder

400 g (13 oz) can chopped tomatoes

125 g (4 oz) tomato purée

600 ml (1 pint) boiling water

dried red chillies, to garnish

1 Place the aubergines in a bowl and stir in the lemon juice.

2 Melt the butter or ghee in a large wok, add the onions, garlic and ginger and fry gently for 4–5 minutes until just soft. Add the black onion seeds, cinnamon, coriander and cumin seeds and stir thoroughly. Fry for a further 2 minutes, then stir in the pepper, salt, garam masala, turmeric and chilli powder.

3 Add the tomatoes with their juices and the tomato purée, stir well and bring to the boil. Pour in the boiling water and stir in the aubergine pieces with the lemon juice. Bring to the boil, lower the heat and simmer gently for 15–20 minutes until soft. Garnish with the dried red chillies and serve hot.

Serves 4–6
Preparation time: 15 minutes
Cooking time: 25–30 minutes

spicy aubergines with tomatoes

leek terrine with walnuts & feta

1 Cut off the roots and most of the green part of the leeks. Split the leeks horizontally to within 5 cm (2 inches) of the root end. Rinse the leaves under running cold water to wash out any grit or mud. Boil the leeks in salted water for 10 minutes or until tender.

2 Fill a 500 g (1 lb) loaf tin with the leeks laid alternately head to tail, sprinkling each layer with salt and pepper. Put a second tin inside the first, pressing down the leeks. Invert both tins so that the water can drain out. Chill for at least 4 hours with a 1 kg (2 lb) weight on top.

3 Carefully turn out the leek terrine. Using a very sharp knife, cut it into six thick slices. Lay each slice on a plate and surround with the salad leaves. Scatter the walnuts and crumbled feta cheese on top of the salad leaves.

4 To make the dressing, combine all the ingredients in a small bowl, season with salt and pepper, then spoon it over the salad. Garnish with the parsley and chives.

20 small young leeks

radicchio or other salad leaves

50 g (2 oz) walnuts, chopped

75 g (3 oz) feta cheese, crumbled

salt and pepper

Dressing:

4 tablespoons olive oil

2 tablespoons walnut oil

2 tablespoons wine vinegar

2 tablespoons English mustard

To Garnish:

flat leaf parsley sprigs

chives

Serves 6

Preparation time: 25 minutes, plus chilling

Cooking time: 10 minutes

50 g (2 oz) butter

1 tablespoon chopped herbs, such as mint and parsley

4 courgettes, cut in half lengthways

2 leeks, trimmed, washed and sliced

2 large carrots, cut into thick matchsticks

125 g (4 oz) French beans, topped and tailed

4 celery sticks, cut into thick matchsticks

1 small bunch of watercress, trimmed

salt and pepper

1 Mix the butter with the herbs and season well with salt and pepper. Place the courgettes, leeks, carrots, beans and celery in a steamer, then season well with salt and pepper.

2 Cover and steam over boiling water for 3–5 minutes. Add the watercress and steam for 1 minute more. Turn on to a warmed serving dish and dot with the herb butter.

Serves 4

Preparation time: 20 minutes

Cooking time: 5 minutes

seasonal vegetable medley

wild mushrooms in crispy cases

1 Brush both sides of the bread with the butter. Press firmly into 8 tartlet or bun tins and bake in a preheated oven, 200°C (400°F), Gas Mark 6, for 10–15 minutes, until crisp and golden brown.

2 Meanwhile, make the filing. Melt the butter in a small saucepan, add the shallot and fry for about 5 minutes until softened. Add the mushrooms and cook for a further 5 minutes, until tender. Stir in the Madeira and allow to bubble briefly, then stir in the cream and chopped parsley, with salt and pepper to taste. Cook over a moderate heat for a few minutes, until the mixture forms a sauce.

3 Arrange the salad leaves on small plates and place a bread case on each one. Fill with the mushroom mixture and serve warm.

Crispy Cases:

8 thin slices of bread, crusts removed

50 g (2 oz) butter, melted

Filling:

25 g (1 oz) butter

1 shallot, chopped

175 g (6 oz) mushrooms (chestnut, oyster, shiitake), sliced

1 tablespoon Madeira

4 tablespoons double cream

1 tablespoon chopped parsley

salt and pepper

assorted salad leaves, to serve

Serves 6–8

Preparation time: 15 minutes

Cooking time: 10–15 minutes

1 Grease a 600 ml (1 pint) loaf tin with butter and line with greased greaseproof paper large enough to extend up the sides. Cook the carrots and beans in separate saucepans in 1 cm (1½ inch) of boiling water until tender. Cook the spinach in a dry saucepan for 3–4 minutes.

2 Drain the vegetables thoroughly, reserving the water, then purée separately, adding 1 egg yolk to each mixture. Add the cream to the puréed broad beans. Season with salt and pepper, and add a little nutmeg to the spinach purée. Spoon the spinach into the prepared tin, levelling to make a smooth layer. Carefully spoon the broad bean purée in an even layer on top, and finally add the carrot purée. Cover with foil and bake in a preheated oven, 160°C (325°F), Gas Mark 3, for 1 hour, removing the foil after about 45 minutes. The pâté should be firm in the centre when touched lightly; leave to cool in the tin.

3 To make the sauce, put the pepper under a hot grill until the skin is blackened and blistered all over. Then place in cold water and peel off the skin. Remove the stalk and rinse away the seeds. Purée in a blender with 200 ml (7 fl oz) of the reserved cooking water. Season to taste, and chill until ready to serve.

4 Slip a knife round the sides of the pâté to loosen it, then turn out of the tin and strip off the greaseproof paper. Cut into slices and place one on each plate on top of a pool of sauce. Garnish with dill and the lime twists.

vegetable terrine

butter, for greasing

250 g (8 oz) carrots, cut into even-sized pieces

250 g (8 oz) broad beans, shelled

250 g (8 oz) frozen spinach, defrosted

3 egg yolks

3 tablespoons double cream

freshly grated nutmeg

salt and pepper

Sauce:

1 large red pepper

To Garnish:

dill sprigs

lime twists

Serves 6

Preparation time: 40 minutes

Cooking time: 1½ hours

camembert & cranberry pie

1 Place the cranberries in a small saucepan with the sugar, water and port. Bring to the boil, then lower the heat and simmer gently until the cranberries pop and are just tender. This should take about 5 minutes. Leave to cool.

2 Layer the filo pastry on a greased baking sheet, brushing each layer with melted butter and arranging each sheet at a slightly different angle from the previous one, to form points all around the edge. Place the Camembert in the centre and spread the cranberry sauce over the top. Season with pepper.

3 Gather up the filo pastry over the cheese and cranberry mixture, scrunching the edges together. Brush with the remaining butter and bake in a preheated oven, 200°C (400°F), Gas Mark 6, for 15–20 minutes, until golden. Cool the pie on the baking sheet for 5 minutes then cut into wedges to serve.

■ Fresh cranberries will keep well in the refrigerator for up to 4 weeks in an unopened bag, or for about 1 week once opened, but remove damaged fruit first.

75 g (3 oz) cranberries

25 g (1 oz) sugar

3 tablespoons water

1 tablespoon port

8 sheets of filo pastry

25 g (1 oz) butter, melted

1 whole Camembert cheese, about 250 g (8 oz)

pepper

Serves 4

Preparation time: 20 minutes

Cooking time: 15–20 minutes

tagliatelle with mushrooms & cream

1 Put the porcini in a bowl, cover with the warm water and leave to soak for 20–30 minutes. Drain, reserving the liquid, then chop into small pieces.

2 Heat the butter in a large pan and fry the garlic and onion until soft, then add the porcini and fry gently for a few minutes. Stir in 3 tablespoons of the reserved liquid and add the field mushrooms. Cover the pan, turn up the heat so the mushrooms produce their own juices and cook, stirring occasionally, until the mushrooms are soft, then add the cream, season with salt and pepper and heat through.

3 Meanwhile, bring a large pan of lightly salted water to the boil, add the tagliatelle and cook for about 10–12 minutes, or according to packet instructions, until just tender.

4 Drain, and turn the pasta into a warmed serving dish. Reheat the sauce, pour over the pasta and garnish with chives.

■ If dried cep mushrooms (porcini) are not available, use fresh ceps which will last for up to 1 week if refrigerated.

15 g (½ oz) dried porcini mushrooms

450 ml (¾ pint) warm water

40 g (1½ oz) butter

1 garlic clove, crushed

50 g (2 oz) onion, finely chopped

375 g (12 oz) field mushrooms, finely sliced

150 ml (¼ pint) double cream

300–375 g (10–12 oz) tagliatelle

butter, to taste

salt and pepper

1 tablespoon chopped chives, to garnish

Serves 3

Preparation time: 10 minutes, plus soaking

Cooking time: 15–20 minutes

wild mushroom salad with croûtons

1 To prepare the mushrooms, leave small ones whole but slice or chop the larger ones.

2 To make the croûtons, cut the bread into small cubes. Heat the oil with the butter in a frying pan until sizzling. Add the bread cubes and fry, stirring constantly, for 3–4 minutes until crisp and golden. Drain on kitchen paper and sprinkle with salt to taste.

3 Heat the olive oil in a large frying pan. Add the shallot and cook over a moderate heat for 3–4 minutes, until softened. Stir in the garlic and cook for a further 1 minute. Add the mushrooms and thyme, season with salt and pepper and cook, stirring, for 2 minutes. Add the water and cook over a moderate heat, stirring frequently, for about 5 minutes or until the mushrooms are tender. Transfer to a bowl and leave to cool.

4 When the mushroom mixture has cooled add the rocket or watercress, basil and croûtons to the bowl. Toss lightly to mix. Drizzle the dressing over the salad and serve sprinkled with chopped parsley, if liked.

500 g (1 lb) mixed wild mushrooms or cultivated mushrooms

4 tablespoons olive oil

1 shallot, finely chopped

1 garlic clove, chopped

1 teaspoon chopped thyme

4 tablespoons water

about 50 g (2 oz) rocket or watercress

handful of basil leaves, roughly torn

6 tablespoons French dressing

chopped parsley, to garnish (optional)

salt and pepper

Croûtons:

3 thick slices of white bread, crusts removed

2 tablespoons light olive oil

25 g (1 oz) butter

Serves 4

Preparation time: 15 minutes

Cooking time: about 12 minutes

guinea fowl with fresh gnocchi •

duck with orange •

braised pheasant with marsala & chestnuts •

chicken with artichokes •

tandoori chicken •

balti chicken vindaloo •

spicy duck in port with fresh figs •

roast pheasant flambéed with calvados •

chicken in red wine •

burgundy-style beef •

beef & new potato salad •

lamb & apricot tagine •

noisettes of lamb with pomegranate •

tournedos en croûte •

fillet steak with smoked oysters •

roghan ghosht •

poultry & meat

1 Roll the guinea fowl in the flour, shaking off any excess. Heat the oil in a large flameproof casserole over a moderate heat, add the guinea fowl, in batches, and brown well. Remove with a slotted spoon and set aside. Reduce the heat, add the shallots, garlic and sage and cook gently for 5 minutes until soft. Add the wine and bring to the boil, stirring. Return the guinea fowl to the casserole with the stock and bay leaf. Bring back to the boil, reduce the heat, cover and simmer for 25–30 minutes.

2 To make the gnocchi, place the potatoes in a pan of water, bring to the boil and cook for 20–25 minutes. Drain well and peel. While still warm, purée in a food processor or press though a sieve into a bowl. Beat the egg and parsley into the mixture. Add the flour slowly (you may not need it all) until smooth and slightly sticky. Season with salt. Roll the mixture into a long sausage about 1 cm (½ inch) in diameter. Cut into 1.5 cm (¾ inch) lengths. Take one piece at a time and press it on to a floured fork. Roll along the prongs and off the fork on to a floured tray. Set aside.

3 To cook the mushrooms, gently melt the butter in a pan, add the shallot and cook until soft. Add the mushrooms, lemon rind and juice and cook until soft. Stir into the casserole 10 minutes before the end of cooking.

4 Bring a large pan of water to the boil and drop in 20–25 pieces of gnocchi at a time. They will quickly rise. Cook for 10–15 seconds. When ready, drain and keep warm while cooking the rest. Serve with the hot casserole.

1 plump guinea fowl, cut into 8 pieces

2 tablespoons seasoned flour

2 tablespoons olive oil

2 shallots, finely chopped

1 garlic clove, crushed

2 tablespoons chopped sage

250 ml (8 fl oz) dry white wine

250 ml (8 fl oz) chicken stock

1 bay leaf

salt and pepper

Gnocchi:

750 g (1½ lb) large potatoes, unpeeled

1 egg, beaten

3 tablespoons chopped parsley

125 g (4 oz) plain flour, sifted

Mushrooms:

50 g (2 oz) butter

1 shallot, finely chopped

500 g (1 lb) mixed mushrooms, cut into halves or quarters if large

finely grated rind of 1 lemon

2 tablespoons lemon juice

Serves 4
Preparation time: 1 hour
Cooking time: 1 hour

guinea fowl with fresh gnocchi

duck with orange

1 Heat the butter and oil in a deep flameproof casserole and add the duck. Fry over a moderate heat, turning the duck as necessary, until it is golden brown all over.

2 Add the garlic and gammon to the casserole and fry for about 1–2 minutes. Add the white wine and stock, bring to the boil, then simmer for 3–4 minutes, or until slightly reduced. Add the bouquet garni and orange juice, season with salt and pepper, then cover the casserole. Reduce the heat and simmer gently, basting occasionally, for 1½ hours or until the duck is cooked.

3 Meanwhile, using a sharp knife, cut the orange rind into fine strips and blanch for 5 minutes in a small pan of boiling water. Remove and drain, then dry thoroughly on kitchen paper and set aside.

4 Blend the flour and butter in a bowl. Remove the duck from the casserole, cut it into serving pieces and keep warm. Boil the cooking liquid for about 10 minutes, until reduced. Add the vinegar, orange rind and little pieces of the flour and butter mixture, stirring constantly, until the sauce thickens. Serve the duck with the sauce, garnished with orange slices and watercress.

25 g (1 oz) butter

3 tablespoons olive oil

2 kg (4 lb) duck, trussed with string

4 garlic cloves, crushed

125 g (4 oz) gammon, cut into thin strips

600 ml (1 pint) dry white wine

200 ml (7 fl oz) chicken stock

1 bouquet garni

rind and juice of 2 oranges

1 tablespoon wine vinegar

1 tablespoon flour

25 g (1 oz) butter, softened

salt and pepper

To Garnish:

2 oranges, thinly sliced

watercress sprigs

Serves 6
Preparation time: 10 minutes
Cooking time: 1¾ hours

braised pheasant with marsala & chestnuts

1 Melt the butter in a large flameproof casserole over a moderate heat, brown the pheasant all over, then transfer the bird to a plate. Reduce the heat, add the bacon and cook for 1 minute. Add the onion, celery and carrot and cook until the onion has softened.

2 Return the pheasant to the pan and add the sage, Marsala and stock. Season with salt and pepper, bring to the boil, cover and simmer gently for 35–40 minutes, adding the chestnuts after 20–25 minutes. Alternatively cook in a preheated oven, 160°C (325°F), Gas Mark 3.

3 To make the beetroot straws, peel the beetroot and slice into very thin rounds, then cut the rounds into very fine julienne strips. Place on kitchen paper and leave to dry out for 30 minutes. Pat dry well. Heat the oil to 180–190° (350–375°F), or until a cube of bread browns in 30 seconds. Cook the beetroot strips in batches until crisp, then drain on kitchen paper.

4 Remove the pheasant from the casserole and keep warm. Skim off any excess fat from the surface. Place the casserole over the heat and boil rapidly until the sauce reduces and thickens slightly. Adjust the seasoning, then serve the sauce with the pheasant, accompanied by the beetroot straws.

25 g (1 oz) butter

1 pheasant, about 1–1.25 kg (2–2¼ lb)

125 g (4 oz) pancetta or streaky bacon, cut into strips

1 large onion, chopped

1 celery stick, chopped

1 large carrot, chopped

1 tablespoon chopped sage

125 ml (4 fl oz) Marsala

500 ml (17 fl oz) chicken stock

250 g (8 oz) vacuum-packed cooked chestnuts

salt and pepper

Beetroot Straws:

250 g (8 oz) raw beetroot

oil, for deep-frying

Serves 4

Preparation time: 30 minutes, plus drying the beetroot straws

---

Cooking time: 1–1½ hours

chicken with artichokes

1 To prepare the artichokes, remove the hard outer leaves then peel back the centre leaves so you can cut out each choke. With a sharp knife, remove the stems of the artichokes. Have ready a large bowl of water and add the lemon juice. Immerse the prepared artichokes in this acidulated water for at least 30 minutes. Remove and drain.

2 Heat the oil in a large sauté pan and gently fry the artichokes and small onions for about 15 minutes, until golden. Add the chicken breasts to the pan and fry for a few minutes on each side, until golden brown. Add the garlic, herbs and wine, and cook over a low heat for 10–15 minutes, until the chicken is cooked through.

3 Remove the chicken, artichokes and onions and keep warm. Increase the heat and boil the pan juices, scraping the bottom of the pan with a wooden spoon to lift all the deposits, until thickened and reduced. Season to taste and pour over the chicken. Garnish with the parsley and serve at once.

8 small young artichokes

4 tablespoons lemon juice

75 ml (3 fl oz) olive oil

250 g (8 oz) small pickling onions, peeled

4 boneless, skinless chicken breasts

3 garlic cloves

thyme sprigs

1 bay leaf

200 ml (7 fl oz) dry white wine

salt and pepper

2 tablespoons chopped flat leaf parsley, to garnish

Serves 4

Preparation time: 15 minutes, plus soaking

Cooking time: 35–40 minutes

■ Soaking the artichokes, or any other vegetable or fruit, in acidulated water helps to prevent discolouration.

tandoori chicken

1 Trim the chicken, leaving the skin on, and make three slashes on each thigh. Arrange the thighs in a single layer in a non-metallic dish. Combine the yogurt and tandoori paste and coat the chicken. Cover and leave to marinate for 30 minutes.

2 Heat the butter or ghee in a large heavy-based pan. Add the ginger and onion and cook until golden. Stir in the mint and fresh coriander and cook for 30 seconds, then remove the mixture and set aside.

3 Add the garlic, ground coriander and cumin to the pan and cook over a moderate heat for 1 minute. Add the chicken thighs, in batches if necessary, and cook on each side for 3 minutes. Return all the thighs to the pan, skin side up, add the stock and bring slowly to the boil. Reduce the heat, cover and simmer for 25 minutes. Remove the lid and cook for a further 10–12 minutes.

4 Spoon the onion mixture over the chicken and cook for about 1 minute until hot. Serve with a spoonful of the sauce and lemon or lime wedges.

■ To make pure ghee, melt 250 g (8 oz) butter in a saucepan, simmer for 10-12 minutes. When the froth turns golden, strain. Store in a jar.

6 chicken thighs or other pieces

50 ml (2 fl oz) natural yogurt

50 ml (2 fl oz) tandoori paste

25 g (1 oz) butter or ghee

5 cm (2 inch) piece of fresh root ginger, peeled and cut into thin strips

1 red onion, cut into thin wedges

25 g (1 oz) mint, chopped

25 g (1 oz) fresh coriander, chopped

2 garlic cloves, chopped

1 teaspoon ground coriander

1 teapoon ground cumin

175 ml (6 fl oz) chicken stock

lemon or lime wedges, to garnish

Serves 4

Preparation time: 10 minutes, plus marinating

Cooking time: about 45 minutes

1½ teaspoons coriander seeds

1½ teaspoons cumin seeds

¼ teaspoon black onion seeds

¼ teaspoon fenugreek seeds

¼ teaspoon mustard seeds

2.5 cm (1 inch) piece of cinnamon stick

3 cloves

¾ teaspoon peppercorns

2 tablespoons desiccated coconut

2 tablespoons unsalted peanuts

6 tablespoons vinegar

2 garlic cloves, crushed

1 teaspoon chopped fresh root ginger

½ teaspoon ground turmeric

1½ teaspoons chilli powder

2 teaspoons salt

1.5 kg (3 lb) chicken, skinned and cut into pieces

3 tablespoons vegetable oil

12 curry leaves, plus extra, to garnish

1 teaspoon cumin seeds

fried onion rings, to garnish

1 Dry roast the coriander, cumin, black onion, fenugreek, mustard, cinnamon, cloves, peppercorns, coconut and peanuts, then grind them in a spice grinder. Transfer to a bowl, then mix in the vinegar, garlic, ginger, turmeric, chilli powder and salt. Spread the mixture over the chicken pieces, cover and leave to marinate overnight.

2 Heat the oil in a balti pan or wok, then add the curry leaves and cumin seeds. Cook for a further 10 seconds, then add the chicken and cook for 15 minutes, turning once or twice. Cover and cook for a further 15–20 minutes or until the chicken is tender, adding a little water from time to time to keep the chicken moist. Leave over a very low heat for a few minutes before serving, garnished with the onion rings and some shredded curry leaves.

Serves 4–6
Preparation time: 20 minutes, plus marinating
Cooking time: 30–40 minutes

balti chicken vindaloo

spicy duck in port with fresh figs

1 Place the duck in a large bowl, add the marinade ingredients, stir well, cover and leave in the refrigerator to marinate for at least 2 hours or overnight.

2 Remove the duck from the marinade, reserving the marinade, and pat dry. Heat a large flameproof casserole over a moderate heat, add the duck, in batches, skin side down first, and brown all over. Transfer each batch to a colander to drain. Pour off most of the fat that has rendered from the duck, leaving about 1 tablespoon.

3 Add the onion and garlic to the casserole and cook gently for 5 minutes until softened. Return the duck pieces, pour in the marinade, bring to the boil and add the stock. Bring back to the boil, reduce the heat and season. Cover with a tight-fitting lid and simmer for 45 minutes. Remove the lid, skim off any fat and lay the figs on top. Cover and cook for a further 20–30 minutes until the meat and figs are tender.

4 Remove the meat and figs from the casserole and keep warm. Discard the star anise, cinnamon, bay leaf and thyme. Skim off as much fat as possible. Increase the heat and boil rapidly until the sauce is reduced by half. Serve the duck with the sauce spooned over.

2 kg (4 lb) duck, cut into 8 pieces

1 onion, chopped

1–2 garlic cloves, crushed

500 ml (17 fl oz) chicken stock

12 ripe figs

salt and pepper

Marinade:

400 ml (14 fl oz) port

4 whole star anise

5 cm (2 inch) piece of cinnamon stick

4 cloves

8 Szechuan or black peppercorns

2 tablespoons chopped stem ginger

4 tablespoons clear honey

1 piece orange or tangerine peel

1 bay leaf

1 thyme sprig

Serves 4

Preparation time: 30 minutes, plus marinating

Cooking time: 1½ hours

roast pheasant flambéed with calvados

1 Place the pheasant in a roasting tin. Tuck the onion halves under the bird and sprinkle with a little salt and pepper. Dot with the butter, place in a preheated oven, 190°C (375°F), Gas Mark 5, and roast for about 45 minutes, or until the pheasant is cooked through and tender, adding the apples 15–20 minutes before the end of the cooking.

2 Transfer the pheasant to a warmed serving dish. Place the apple slices in a separate dish and keep them hot while making the sauce.

3 Stir the flour into the pan juices and cook over a moderate heat for 1 minute. Stir in the wine and bring to the boil, stirring all the time. Remove from the heat. Heat the Calvados in a small saucepan until it is just warm, set it alight and then, when the flames die down, add it to the sauce. Stir in the double cream and chopped parsley. Taste for seasoning, then reheat the sauce without boiling.

4 Pour a little of the sauce around the pheasant and arrange the apples in the dish. Serve with roast potatoes and vegetables, with the remaining sauce served separately.

1 oven-ready pheasant, preferably a hen bird

1 small onion, halved

25 g (1 oz) butter

2 tart dessert apples, peeled, cored and thickly sliced

salt and pepper

Sauce:

15 g (½ oz) plain flour

150 ml (¼ pint) dry white wine

2 tablespoons Calvados

50 ml (2 fl oz) double cream

1 tablespoon chopped parsley

salt and pepper

Serves 2

Preparation time: 20 minutes

Cooking time: 45 minutes

chicken in red wine

1 Heat the oil and butter in a large heavy-based pan and add the chicken pieces. Fry over a low heat until golden on all sides, turning occasionally. Remove the chicken from the pan with a slotted spoon and keep warm. Pour off a little of the fat, then add the pickling onions and bacon and fry until lightly coloured, then sprinkle in the flour and stir well.

2 Pour in the wine and bring to the boil, stirring. Add the bouquet garni, unpeeled garlic cloves, sugar, nutmeg, and salt and pepper to taste. Return the chicken to the casserole, lower the heat, cover and simmer for 15 minutes.

3 Add the mushrooms and cook gently for a further 45 minutes or until the chicken pieces are cooked and just tender. Remove with a slotted spoon and arrange on a warmed serving plate. Keep hot. Pour the brandy into the sauce and boil, uncovered, for 15 minutes until thick and reduced. Remove and discard the bouquet garni and garlic cloves.

4 Pour the sauce over the chicken and garnish with chopped parsley. Serve with some fried bread triangles to mop up the sauce, if liked.

2 tablespoons oil

50 g (2 oz) butter

2.5 kg (5 lb) chicken, cut into 12 pieces

24 small pickling onions, peeled

125 g (4 oz) piece of smoked bacon, diced

1 tablespoon plain flour

1 bottle Burgundy or other good red wine

1 bouquet garni

2 garlic cloves, unpeeled

a pinch of sugar

freshly grated nutmeg

24 button mushrooms

1 tablespoon brandy

salt and pepper

2 tablespoons finely chopped parsley, to garnish

fried bread triangles, to serve (optional)

Serves 6–8

Preparation time: 15–20 minutes

Cooking time: 1½ hours

---

burgundy-style beef

1 large onion, thinly sliced

a few parsley sprigs

a few thyme sprigs

1 bay leaf, crushed

1 kg (2 lb) chuck steak or top rump, cut into chunks

2 tablespoons brandy

400 ml (14 fl oz) red Burgundy or other good red wine

2 tablespoons olive oil

50 g (2 oz) butter

150 g (5 oz) lean bacon, roughly chopped

24 small pickling onions, peeled

500 g (1 lb) button mushrooms, halved

25 g (1 oz) plain flour

300 ml (½ pint) beef or chicken stock

1 garlic clove, crushed

1 bouquet garni

salt and pepper

Serves 4–6

Preparation time: 30 minutes, plus marinating

Cooking time: 2½ hours

1 Put a few onion slices in a deep bowl with a little parsley, thyme and some crumbled bay leaf. Place a few pieces of beef on top, and continue layering up in this way, until all the onion, beef and herbs are used. Mix the brandy with the wine and oil, and pour over the beef. Cover and leave to marinate for at least 4 hours.

2 Melt the butter in a flameproof casserole, add the bacon and fry over a moderate heat until golden brown. Remove and set aside. Add the small onions and fry until golden all over. Remove and set aside. Add the mushrooms and fry, stirring, for about 1 minute. Drain and set aside.

3 Remove the beef from the marinade, then strain the marinade and set aside. Add the beef to the casserole and fry briskly until browned. Sprinkle in the flour and cook, stirring, for 1 minute. Gradually stir in the strained marinade, then add the stock, garlic and bouquet garni. Season to taste, cover and simmer gently for 2 hours.

4 Skim off any fat on the surface, and add the bacon, onions and mushrooms to the casserole. Cover and simmer for 30 minutes, or until the beef is tender. Discard the bouquet garni and serve immediately.

beef & new potato salad

1 Cook the pepper halves skin-side up under a preheated hot grill for about 10–15 minutes, without turning, until the skin is blackened and blistered all over. Transfer to a bowl, cover with kitchen paper and set aside, then rub off and discard the charred skin; cut the flesh into strips. Set aside.

2 Season the beef liberally with pepper. Grill for about 5 minutes, turning once, until well browned on the outside but still rare on the inside. Transfer to a plate and leave to cool.

3 Cut the potatoes in half. Place in a bowl with the pepper strips, French beans, onion, tomatoes and olives. Slice the beef thinly, cutting across the grain, and add to the bowl with the thyme. Season with salt and pepper to taste.

4 Combine all the ingredients for the dressing in a screw-top jar and shake well. Spoon over the salad and toss lightly.

1 red pepper, halved, cored and deseeded

375 g (12 oz) beef fillet, cut into 2.5 cm (1 inch) steaks

500 g (1 lb) small new potatoes, boiled and cooled

125 g (4 oz) French beans, cooked and cooled

½ red onion, thinly sliced

125 g (4 oz) red and yellow cherry tomatoes, halved

about 16 anchovy-stuffed green olives

a few black olives (optional)

2 teaspoons chopped thyme

salt and pepper

Sweet Mustard Dressing:

3 tablespoons olive oil

2 tablespoons wholegrain mustard

1 tablespoon clear honey

1 teaspoon lemon juice

Serves 4–6
Preparation time: 30 minutes
Cooking time: about 25 minutes

lamb & apricot tagine

1 Place the meat in a large flameproof casserole and add the onion, garlic, all the spices and lemon rind and juice. Mix well and add the water to cover. Bring to the boil, then reduce the heat, cover the casserole and simmer for 1 hour.

2 Stir in the honey, apricots and parsley, season with salt and pepper to taste, and cook, covered, for a further 30 minutes until the lamb is tender.

3 Meanwhile, heat the oil in a frying pan, add the almonds and cook, shaking the pan occasionally, for 5 minutes until evenly golden.

4 When the meat is cooked, if the sauce is too thin, remove the meat with a slotted spoon and keep warm while you boil the sauce, uncovered, until it reduces to the required consistency. Sprinkle the tagine with the almonds and serve with couscous or rice.

1 kg (2 lb) boneless lean lamb, trimmed and cut into 2.5 cm (1 inch) cubes

1 large onion, chopped

2 garlic cloves, crushed

1 teaspoon ground coriander

1 teaspoon ground cumin

½ teaspoon ground cinnamon

¼ teaspoon ground ginger

pinch of saffron threads

2 thin strips of lemon rind

2 tablespoons fresh lemon juice

about 600–900 ml (1–1½ pints) water

1–2 tablespoons honey

250 g (8 oz) dried apricots, soaked in warm water for 2 hours or overnight

1 tablespoon chopped flat leaf parsley

1 tablespoon olive oil

50 g (2 oz) whole blanched almonds

salt and pepper

Serves 4

Preparation time: 20 minutes, plus soaking

Cooking time: 1½ hours

12 noisettes of lamb

1 pomegranate, halved

3 spring onions, finely chopped

½ teaspoon black peppercorns, lightly crushed

150 ml (¼ pint) lamb or beef stock

150 ml (¼ pint) red wine

parsley sprigs, to garnish

noisettes of lamb with pomegranate

Serves 6

Preparation time: 15 minutes, plus marinating

Cooking time: about 20 minutes

1 Trim any excess fat from the noisettes and put them in a shallow dish, in one layer. Using a lemon squeezer, squeeze the juice from the pomegranate and pour it over the lamb. Add the spring onions and peppercorns. Cover and leave to marinate for at least 2 hours. Drain the noisettes, reserving the marinade, and dry them on kitchen paper.

2 In a non-stick pan, fry the lamb noisettes without added fat to seal them on both sides. Pour over the stock and red wine. Simmer, uncovered, until the liquid has reduced by about half. Add the reserved marinade and bring to the boil.

3 Remove the noisettes from the pan with a slotted spoon and arrange them on a warmed serving plate. Garnish with parsley sprigs. Pour over the sauce and serve with new potatoes and a green vegetable.

■ Pomegranates are usually only available for a limited season during the winter months, but they are excellent served with some of the richer meats and help to tenderize the flesh too.

1 Heat half the butter and the oil in a frying pan and gently cook the onion and garlic until soft. Add the mushrooms and nutmeg, and season with salt and pepper. Stir over a gentle heat until the mushrooms are cooked and the moisture has evaporated. Remove from the pan, divide into 4 portions and leave to cool.

2 Heat the remaining butter in a clean frying pan, add the fillet steaks and sear quickly on both sides. Remove from the pan, cool quickly and keep chilled until required.

3 Roll out the pastry on a lightly floured surface and cut into 4 rounds large enough to half-cover the steaks. Brush a 2.5 cm (1 inch) border around the edge of each pastry with beaten egg. Cut the ham into 4 rounds the same size as the steaks.

4 Place 1 piece of ham on each of 2 pastry rounds. Cover the ham with a portion of the mushroom mixture, a fillet steak, another portion of mushrooms and another round of ham. Top with a pastry circle. Seal the edges of the pastry between your fingers and then with a fork. Cut any pastry trimmings into leaves and use to decorate the croûtes. Brush with beaten egg and cook in a preheated oven, 220°C (425°F), Gas Mark 7, for 20 minutes until golden brown. Serve with new potatoes and asparagus.

25 g (1 oz) butter

1 tablespoon oil

1 small onion, finely chopped

1 garlic clove, crushed

50 g (2 oz) mushrooms, finely chopped

pinch of ground nutmeg

2 fillet steaks, about 175 g (6 oz) each, trimmed

125 g (4 oz) fresh or frozen puff pastry, defrosted

1 egg, beaten

2 slices of ham

salt and pepper

Serves 2

Preparation time: 20 minutes

Cooking time: 30–35 minutes

tournedos en croûte

fillet steak with smoked oysters

1 Carefully cut three-quarters through each steak and open out butterfly-style. Place between 2 sheets of greaseproof paper and beat with a rolling pin to an even thickness.

2 Season with salt and pepper and brush lightly with a little oil. Place under a preheated hot grill and cook for 6–10 minutes.

3 Meanwhile, heat the remaining oil in a pan and sauté the onions and mushrooms for about 5 minutes until soft. Add the wine, stock and tomato purée and simmer for about 3–4 minutes, until the liquid is slightly reduced and thickened. Add the drained oysters.

4 Spoon the sauce over the steaks and garnish with watercress.

300 g (10 oz) beef fillet cut into 2 steaks

1 tablespoon soya or sunflower oil

50 g (2 oz) onions, finely sliced

75 g (3 oz) button mushrooms, finely sliced

25 ml (1 fl oz) red wine

25 ml (1 fl oz) beef or chicken stock

1 tablespoon tomato purée

50 g (2 oz) canned smoked oysters, drained

salt and pepper

watercress, to garnish

Serves 2
Preparation time: 15 minutes
Cooking time: 15–20 minutes

roghan ghosht

1 Heat 2 tablespoons of the oil in a large saucepan, add half of the onions and fry until golden. Add the lamb and 175 g (6 oz) of the yogurt, stir well, then cover and simmer for 20 minutes.

2 Meanwhile, put the garlic, ginger, chillies, coriander seeds, cumin seeds, mint, fresh coriander and 2–3 tablespoons of the yogurt in a food processor or blender and work to a smooth paste.

3 Heat the remaining oil in a large saucepan, add the cardamom, cloves and cinnamon and fry quickly for 1 minute, stirring. Add the remaining onion and the prepared spice paste and fry for 5 minutes, stirring constantly. Add the lamb and yogurt mixture, season to taste, stir well and bring to simmering point. Cover and cook for 30 minutes.

4 Add the almonds and cook for a further 15 minutes, until the meat is tender. Remove the whole spices before serving. Garnish with fried onion rings and lemon slices and serve immediately.

4 tablespoons oil

2 onions, finely chopped

750 g (1½ lb) boned leg of lamb, cubed

300 g (10 oz) natural yogurt

2 garlic cloves

2.5 cm (1 inch) piece of fresh root ginger, peeled and roughly chopped

2 green chillies, seeded

1 tablespoon coriander seeds

1 teaspoon cumin seeds

1 teaspoon chopped mint leaves

1 teaspoon chopped coriander

6 cardamom pods, crushed

6 cloves

2.5 cm (1 inch) piece of cinnamon stick

125 g (4 oz) flaked almonds

salt and pepper

To Garnish:

fried onion rings

lemon slices

Serves 4
Preparation time: 20 minutes
Cooking time: about 1¼ hours

ginger cake ●

tarte tatin ●

champagne summer berries ●

chocolate & cinnamon bread & butter pudding ●

chocolate truffles ●

chocolate & orange roulade ●

chocolate chip ice cream ●

exotic fruit salad ●

lemon tart ●

red fruit salad with coeurs à la crème ●

desserts

ginger cake

1   Line and grease an 18 cm (7 inch) cake tin. Cream the fat and sugar together in a mixing bowl until light and fluffy. Add the eggs one at a time, adding a tablespoon of flour with the last two. Sift and fold in the remaining flour and the ground ginger, then fold in the preserved ginger and syrup.

2   Turn the mixture into the prepared cake tin and bake in a preheated oven, 180°C (350°F), Gas Mark 4, for 1–1½ hours. Turn out on to a wire rack to cool.

3   To make the ginger icing, beat the icing sugar and syrup together until smooth. Pour over the cake and leave until set. Decorate the cake with ginger strips.

175 g (6 oz) butter or margarine

175 g (6 oz) caster sugar

3 eggs

250 g (8 oz) self-raising flour

½ teaspoon ground ginger

75 g (3 oz) preserved ginger, chopped

2 tablespoons ginger syrup

preserved ginger strips, to decorate

Ginger Icing:

175 g (6 oz) icing sugar, sifted

2 tablespoons ginger syrup

Makes one 18 cm (7 inch) cake
Preparation time: 15 minutes
Cooking time: 15–20 minutes

tarte tatin

1 Place the flour in a bowl, add the diced butter and rub in with your fingertips until the mixture resembles fine breadcrumbs. Stir in the sugar. Add the egg yolk and enough water, about 2–3 tablespoons, to mix to a firm and smooth dough.

2 To prepare the apple mixture, melt the butter and sugar in a 20 cm (8 inch) ovenproof frying pan. When the mixture is golden, add the apples and toss them in the syrup to coat them. Cook for a few minutes, until the apples start to caramelize.

3 Roll out the pastry on a lightly floured surface to a round, a little larger than the pan. Place it over the apples, folding over the edges of the pastry until it fits the pan neatly.

4 Bake in a preheated oven, 200°C (400°F), Gas Mark 6 for 35–40 minutes, until the pastry is golden. Cool in the pan for 5 minutes, place a large plate on top of the pan and invert the tart on to it. Serve warm with thick cream or crème fraîche served separately, if liked.

thick cream or crème fraîche, to serve

Pastry:

175 g (6 oz) plain flour

75 g (3 oz) chilled butter, diced

25 g (1 oz) caster sugar

1 egg yolk

Apple Mixture:

50 g (2 oz) butter

50 g (2 oz) caster sugar

6 dessert apples, such as Cox's, peeled, cored and quartered

Serves 4–6
Preparation time: 20 minutes
Cooking time: 35–40 minutes

■ A delicious variation is to substitute the apples with 5 pears and sprinkle with 50 g (2 oz) walnut halves before covering with the pastry. Then follow the main recipe.

champagne summer berries

1 Mix all the berries in a pudding basin. Sprinkle them with half of the sugar and half of the lemon juice and set aside for 10 minutes.

2 Meanwhile, pour the remaining sugar on to a large plate. Dip the rims of four glass dessert bowls into the remaining lemon juice, shake off the excess, then dip each dish into the sugar. The sugar will cling to the lemon juice, making an attractive frosted rim.

3 Cover the pudding basin with kitchen foil and tie down. Place in a steamer or covered pan half-filled with boiling water and steam for about 3–5 minutes.

4 To serve, spoon the fruit into the prepared dishes being careful not to spoil the frosted rim. At the table, pour the chilled Champagne on to the fruit and decorate with mint sprigs. Serve with almond biscuits.

250 g (8 oz) strawberries, hulled and halved

250 g (8 oz) raspberries

125 g (4 oz) redcurrants, topped and tailed

125 g (4 oz) blueberries

25 g (1 oz) caster sugar

4 tablespoons lemon juice

250 ml (8 fl oz) chilled Champagne

mint sprigs, to decorate

almond biscuits, to serve

Serves 4

Preparation time: 15 minutes, plus chilling

Cooking time: 3–5 minutes

1 Spread the sliced bread with the butter and sprinkle with the cinnamon. Cut each slice of bread into 4 triangles.

2 Beat the sugar and eggs together in a bowl. Heat the milk, coffee and half of the chocolate to just above room temperature. Whisk until well blended, then pour over the eggs. Mix well.

3 Layer the bread in a lightly greased 900 ml (1½ pint) pie dish and strain over the custard. Leave to stand for at least 30 minutes.

4 Place the dish in a bain-marie, pour about 900 ml (1½) pints of water around the dish and bake in a preheated oven, 180°C (350°F), Gas Mark 4, for 1¼–1½ hours, or until the custard is set. About 10 minutes before the end of cooking time, sprinkle over the remaining chocolate.

4 large slices of bread, crusts removed

25 g (1 oz) butter, softened

1 teaspoon ground cinnamon

40 g (1½ oz) sugar

3 eggs

600 ml (1 pint) milk

1 teaspoon instant coffee powder or granules

75 g (3 oz) plain chocolate, grated

Serves 2

Preparation time: 10 minutes, plus standing

Cooking time: 1¼–1½ hours

chocolate & cinnamon bread & butter pudding

chocolate truffles

1 Heat the cream gently until tepid. Put 125 g (4 oz) of the chocolate pieces into a small bowl and melt gently over hot, but not boiling, water, stirring occasionally. Do not rest the base in the hot water. Remove the bowl from the heat and slowly pour in the cream, stirring thoroughly.

2 Leave the mixture to cool then add the whisky or brandy. Whisk for 3–4 minutes until the mixture is light and stands in peaks. Chill in the refrigerator for about 20 minutes.

3 Sieve the cocoa powder on to a tray. Roll spoonfuls of the chocolate paste into balls about 2.5 cm (1 inch) in diameter then roll them in the cocoa powder to cover. Leave to cool until firm.

4 To cover the truffles in chocolate, melt the remaining chocolate over hot water. Spear each truffle on a skewer and dip them one by one into the melted chocolate. Place on a marble slab or foil to set. Dust with the cocoa powder to serve.

3 tablespoons double cream

325 g (9 oz) plain chocolate, broken into small pieces

½–1 tablespoon whisky or brandy (optional)

2 tablespoons cocoa powder, for dusting

Makes 10 truffles

Preparation time: 40 minutes, plus chilling

---

chocolate & orange roulade

1 In a mixing bowl, whisk the egg yolks and sugar until thick and creamy. Sift the cocoa powder over the mixture and fold in thoroughly. In a second bowl, whisk the egg whites until stiff and gently fold into the chocolate mixture.

2 Spoon into a greased and lined 30 x 20 cm (12 x 8 inch) Swiss roll tin and level the surface. Bake in a preheated oven, 180°C (350°F), Gas Mark 4, for 25–30 minutes or until firm. Cool for 5 minutes, then cover with a damp tea towel and leave until completely cold.

3 Sift the icing sugar over a large sheet of greaseproof paper. Invert the cake on to the paper and carefully peel off the lining paper.

4 Put the double cream into a bowl and whip until thick. Add the fromage frais, icing sugar, orange rind and liqueur. Mix gently. Spread the mixture over the cake, then roll up like a Swiss roll with the help of the greaseproof paper. Transfer the roulade to a serving dish. Dust with more icing sugar if liked, and serve immediately. The cake may crack when rolled but this is quite normal.

4 eggs, separated

175 g (6 oz) caster sugar

40 g (1½ oz) cocoa powder

icing sugar, sifted

Filling:

150 ml (¼ pint) double cream

150 g (5 oz) natural fromage frais

2 tablespoons icing sugar, sifted

finely grated rind of 1 orange

1 tablespoon orange liqueur

Serves 6–8

Preparation time: 30 minutes, plus cooling

Cooking time: 25–30 minutes

chocolate chip ice cream

1 Whip the cream with the caster sugar until it holds its shape on the whisk. Transfer to a freezer tray or a lidded container so that it can be beaten easily. Freeze the cream for 30 minutes, beat thoroughly, then freeze again for a further 30 minutes.

2 Meanwhile, spread the breadcrumbs on a grill pan and sprinkle with the sugar. Place under a preheated grill until the sugar caramelizes. Stir well to ensure even browning. Leave to cool.

3 If necessary, grind or crush the breadcrumbs to break up any lumps. Stir in the hazelnuts.

4 Remove the frozen cream from the freezer and beat thoroughly. Stir in the breadcrumb mixture then the chopped chocolate. Mix well, then return to the freezer for a further 2 hours. If the ice cream has been frozen for 24 hours or longer, remove from the freezer and allow to soften for 1 hour before serving.

600 ml (1 pint) double cream

1 tablespoon caster sugar

125 g (4 oz) fresh brown breadcrumbs

75 g (3 oz) soft dark brown sugar

50 g (2 oz) hazelnuts, chopped and toasted

125 g (4 oz) bitter dessert or plain chocolate, roughly chopped

Makes 600 ml (1 pint)

Preparation time: about 20 minutes, plus freezing

■ Turn your freezer to the fast freeze setting before starting to make this recipe, but don't forget to turn it back to the usual setting afterwards.

1 Cut the top off the pineapple and pull away 2 or 3 leaves. Cut out the flesh of the pineapple by cutting around it with a long sharp knife and scooping out the flesh with a spoon. Slice the flesh into bite-sized pieces, discarding the core.

2 Halve the passion fruit and spoon out the flesh.

3 Mix all the fruits together in a bowl with the kirsch. Spoon them into the pineapple shell and chill.

4 Just before serving, decorate with the pineapple leaves. Serve with yogurt or pouring cream.

1 small pineapple

1 passion fruit

1 kiwi fruit, peeled and sliced

1 mango, peeled and sliced, stone removed

3 tablespoons kirsch

natural yogurt or pouring cream, to serve

Serves 2

Preparation time: 30 minutes, plus cooling

exotic fruit salad

■ To speed up the ripening process of unripe kiwis, place them in a plastic bag with a ripe apple or pear.

lemon tart

250 g (8 oz) plain flour

pinch of salt

125 g (4 oz) butter

1 egg yolk

2–3 tablespoons iced water

Filling:

grated rind and juice of 3 lemons

75 g (3 oz) caster sugar

2 eggs, plus 1 egg white

75 ml (3 fl oz) double cream

125 g (4 oz) ground almonds

a good pinch of ground cinnamon

Topping:

2 lemons, thinly sliced

125 g (4 oz) caster sugar

1 To make the pastry, sift the flour and salt into a bowl and rub in the butter until the mixture resembles breadcrumbs. Stir in the egg yolk and sufficient iced water to make a soft and pliable dough. Chill in the refrigerator for 30 minutes.

2 To make the filling, put the lemon rind and juice, and sugar in a mixing bowl. Break in the eggs and add the egg white. Beat well and then beat in the cream, ground almonds and cinnamon. The mixture should be thick and smooth.

3 Roll out the pastry on a lightly floured surface, and use to line a 25 cm (10 inch) loose-bottomed flan tin. Prick the base with a fork and pour in the filling mixture. Bake in a preheated oven, 190°C (375°F), Gas Mark 5, for 20 minutes, or until it is set and golden. Set aside to cool.

4 To make the topping, heat the lemon slices in a little water over low heat for about 10 minutes, or until tender. Remove and drain the lemon slices, keeping about 75 ml (3 fl oz) of the liquid. Add the sugar and stir over gentle heat until dissolved. Bring to the boil, add the lemon slices and cook rapidly until they are coated with thick syrup. Remove and use to decorate the tart. Leave to cool and serve.

Serves 6–8

Preparation time: 15 minutes, plus chilling

Cooking time: 30 minutes

red fruit salad with coeurs à la crème

1 First make the coeurs à la crème. Sprinkle the gelatine on the water in a small bowl. Stir well then stand the bowl in hot water to dissolve.

2 Beat together the cottage cheese, yogurt and cream, then stir in the dissolved gelatine. Spoon the mixture into 2 heart-shaped draining moulds. Leave overnight.

3 Put half of the raspberries in a food processor and blend to a purée, then press through a sieve. Stir the honey into the purée over a low heat. Stir in the remaining raspberries, the cherries and blackcurrants and simmer gently for 2–3 minutes. Leave to cool, then chill in the refrigerator for at least 1 hour.

4 Gently turn out the moulds and decorate them with a pinch of grated nutmeg. Serve with the red fruit salad arranged around the heart.

375 g (12 oz) raspberries

2 tablespoons clear honey

125 g (4 oz) dessert cherries, pitted

125 g (4 oz) blackcurrants, stripped from stalks

Coeurs à la Crème:

1 teaspoon powdered gelatine

1 tablespoon hot water

175 g (6 oz) cottage cheese, sieved

75 ml (3 fl oz) natural yogurt

2 tablespoons double cream

grated nutmeg

Serves 2

Preparation time: 30 minutes, plus overnight draining and chilling

Cooking time: 5 minutes

96

index